GEORGETOWN ELEMENTARY SCHOOL

3001700100073M

Hurricanes
551.55 OLS

W9-BLO-906

Georgetown Elementary School
Indian Prairie School District
Aurora, Illinois

TITLE I MATERIALS

Weather Update

Hurricanes

by Nathan Olson

Consultant:
Joseph M. Moran, PhD
Associate Director, Education Program
American Meteorological Society
Washington, D.C.

Mankato, Minnesota

Bridgestone Books are published by Capstone Press,
151 Good Counsel Drive, P.O. Box 669, Mankato, Minnesota 56002.
www.capstonepress.com

Copyright © 2006 by Capstone Press. All rights reserved.
No part of this publication may be reproduced in whole or in part, or stored in a retrieval
system, or transmitted in any form or by any means, electronic, mechanical, photocopying,
recording, or otherwise, without written permission of the publisher.
For information regarding permission, write to Capstone Press,
151 Good Counsel Drive, P.O. Box 669, Dept. R, Mankato, Minnesota 56002.
Printed in the United States of America

Library of Congress Cataloging-in-Publication Data
Olson, Nathan.
 Hurricanes / by Nathan Olson.
  p. cm.—(Bridgestone Books. Weather update)
 Summary: "A brief introduction to hurricanes, including what they are, how they form,
and hurricane safety"—Provided by publisher.
 Includes bibliographical references and index.
 ISBN 0-7368-4332-9 (hardcover)
 1. Hurricanes—Juvenile literature. I. Title. II. Series.
QC944.2.O38 2006
551.55'2—dc22   2004029193

Editorial Credits
Jennifer Besel, editor; Molly Nei, set designer; Kate Opseth, book designer; Wanda Winch,
 photo researcher; Scott Thoms, photo editor

Photo Credits
Corbis Sygma/Post and Courier, 18
Cory Langley, 14
Folio, Inc./Michael Ventura, 6
Getty Images Inc./Burton McNeely, cover
The Image Finders/Mark E. Gibson, 20
The Image Works/Jeff Greenberg, 16
Peter Arnold, Inc./Weatherstock, 4, 10
Photodisc/StockTrek, 1, 8
Photri MicroStock/Topham, 12

1 2 3 4 5 6 10 09 08 07 06 05

Table of Contents

What Are Hurricanes? 5

Where Hurricanes Happen 7

How Hurricanes Form 9

Storm Surges 11

Forecasting Hurricanes 13

Measuring Hurricanes 15

Naming Hurricanes 17

Hurricane Safety 19

Major Hurricanes in History 21

Glossary 22

Read More 23

Internet Sites 23

Index 24

What Are Hurricanes?

Wind whips all around. Clouds spin like a giant wheel. Rain falls from the sky. Huge waves splash onto shore.

Hurricanes are powerful ocean storms. Spinning winds, heavy rain, and huge waves make up a hurricane. The center of the storm is called the eye. The eye of the storm is calm. Everything around the eye is wild.

Hurricanes can do great damage. Winds blow down homes and trees. Heavy rain and waves flood cities. Hurricanes can hurt or kill people.

◄ Waves crash onto shore as Hurricane George hits the Florida coast in 1998.

Where Hurricanes Happen

Hurricanes happen all over the world. When they form in the Atlantic Ocean, they can hit the United States. Some of these storms hit states along the East Coast. Other hurricanes blow toward the southern United States. These storms can hit states like Texas and Florida.

In some parts of the world, hurricanes have different names. Hurricanes that form in the Pacific Ocean are called **typhoons**. **Cyclones** are hurricanes that form in the Indian Ocean.

◄ In November 1984, a hurricane caused great damage on the island of St. Kitts in the West Indies.

How Hurricanes Form

Hurricanes start in warm ocean water. Warm, damp air rises from the surface of the ocean. The air cools as it rises. The water in the air **condenses** and forms clouds.

As the water forms clouds, it gives off heat. The storm uses the heat as energy. More air rises and cools. The storm begins to grow and spin. When winds reach speeds of 74 miles (119 kilometers) per hour, the storm has become a hurricane.

◄ This satellite picture shows the spinning clouds of a hurricane moving toward the Florida coast.

Storm Surges

Rushing water from a hurricane's **storm surge** can cause great damage. The winds from the storm make ocean water pile up. The water is pushed toward land, forming a huge dome. As it hits land, a storm surge can flood cities and homes.

In 1969, Hurricane Camille's storm surge hit Mississippi. It was the largest surge ever recorded. Camille's storm surge grew to be 24 feet (7 meters) high. It destroyed almost everything in its path. This storm surge killed at least 100 people.

◄ In September 2004, the storm surge from Hurricane Ivan flooded parts of Pensacola, Florida.

Forecasting Hurricanes

Forecasting hurricanes is not easy. **Forecasters** use pictures taken from space to see where a hurricane is forming.

Some U.S. Air Force pilots are called "hurricane hunters." These pilots fly airplanes into hurricanes. They measure wind speed, **air pressure**, and temperature inside the hurricane. The pilots send the information back to forecasters. Forecasters use the information to tell where the storm might hit.

◄ "Hurricane hunters" fly a plane into a hurricane to measure the storm's strength.

Measuring Hurricanes

Scientists use the Saffir-Simpson Scale to describe the strength of a hurricane. Hurricanes range from category 1 to category 5 storms on the scale.

A category 1 hurricane is the weakest. Winds in this storm blow from 74 to 94 miles (119 to 151 kilometers) per hour. Category 1 storms do the least damage.

The strongest hurricane is a category 5. Its winds reach speeds of at least 155 miles (250 kilometers) per hour. Winds in this storm blow down trees and destroy buildings.

◄ Winds during a category 1 hurricane were strong enough to topple a tree into this newly built home.

Naming Hurricanes

More than one hurricane can form at a time. Forecasters name each hurricane to help people keep track of the storms.

Since the 1970s, forecasters around the world have agreed on names for hurricanes. They use the same list of names every six years. Some hurricanes cause a lot of damage. These hurricanes' names are taken off the list. A new name is added to the list when a name is **retired**.

◄ Forecasters at the National Hurricane Center use hurricane names to help people keep track of approaching storms.

Hurricane Safety

The National Hurricane Center tells people when storms are coming. A hurricane watch means a storm could hit within 36 hours. A warning tells people a hurricane is expected to hit land within 24 hours.

Watches and warnings mean people need to get ready for a storm. They should have food and water to last a week. People should also have flashlights and radios. When a strong storm is coming, people in its path need to leave their homes. They need to go to a safer place to wait for the hurricane to end.

◄ Traffic backs up over 100 miles (161 kilometers) as people try to move out of the path of Hurricane Floyd.

Major Hurricanes in History

In 1992, a category 5 hurricane hit Florida and Louisiana. Hurricane Andrew destroyed businesses and schools. Thousands of people lost their homes. Power lines were blown down. At least 23 people were killed.

The strongest hurricane in the United States hit in September 1935. Wind gusts of 200 miles (322 kilometers) per hour hit the Florida Keys. At least 400 people were killed.

People and property are hurt by hurricanes every year. Hurricanes are some of the most powerful storms on earth.

◄ Hurricane Andrew's strong winds shattered mobile homes and destroyed cars.

Glossary

air pressure (AIR PRESH-ur)—the weight of air on a surface

condense (kon-DENSS)—to change from a vapor to a liquid

cyclone (SYE-klone)—a hurricane that occurs in the
Indian Ocean

forecaster (FOR-kast-ur)—a person who predicts the weather

retire (ri-TIRE)—to remove from use

storm surge (STORM SURJ)—a sudden, strong rush of water
that happens as a hurricane moves onto land

typhoon (tye-FOON)—a hurricane that occurs in the
Pacific Ocean

Read More

Rotter, Charles. *Hurricanes: Storms of the Sea.* LifeViews. Mankato, Minn.: Creative Education, 2003.

Spilsbury, Louise, and Richard Spilsbury. *Howling Hurricanes.* Awesome Forces of Nature. Chicago: Heinemann, 2004.

Internet Sites

FactHound offers a safe, fun way to find Internet sites related to this book. All of the sites on FactHound have been researched by our staff.

Here's how:
1. Visit *www.facthound.com*
2. Type in this special code **0736843329** for age-appropriate sites. Or enter a search word related to this book for a more general search.
3. Click on the **Fetch It** button.

FactHound will fetch the best sites for you!

Index

clouds, 5, 9
cyclones, 7

damage, 5, 7, 11, 15, 17, 21

floods, 5, 11
forecasters, 13, 17
formation of, 7, 9, 13

hurricanes
    Andrew, 21
    Camille, 11
    Floyd, 19
    George, 5
    Ivan, 11
    strongest, 21
hurricane eyes, 5
hurricane hunters, 13

measuring hurricanes, 15

names, 7, 17
National Hurricane Center,
    17, 19

oceans, 7, 9, 11

safety, 19
Saffir-Simpson Scale, 15
storm surges, 11

typhoons, 7

warnings, 19
watches, 19
winds, 5, 9, 11, 13, 15, 21